In the Labyrinth of Grief

In the Labyrinth of Grief

40 Words of God that Offer Comfort

Jos Douma

Translated by Dick Moes

RESOURCE *Publications* · Eugene, Oregon

IN THE LABYRINTH OF GRIEF
40 Words of God that Offer Comfort

Resource Publishing
A Division of Wipf and Stock Publishers
199 W. 8th Ave., Suite 3
Eugene, OR 97401
www.wipfandstock.com

ISBN 13: 978-1-60608-791-6

Manufactured in the U.S.A.

Originally published in Dutch as *In het doolhof van de rouw: 40
bijbelwoorden die troost bieden* by Uitgeverij Kok, Kampen, 2008.

English translation © 2009 by Dick Moes.

Foreword

WE ALL have to deal with loss and grief in our lives since we are mortal human beings. Our health, for which we are thankful, can suddenly turn into sickness. Our plans for our life, which bring us so much happiness, can be overtaken by death—sometimes quite suddenly, sometimes after a long struggle with illness and decreasing strength. How do we deal with this loss and grief?

The texts in this little book were occasioned by the death of three people in my congregation in a period of two months. We traveled the journey together with a fifty-eight-year-old sister who had terminal cancer. During that time, quite unexpectedly a fifty-four-year-old brother died because of a heart attack. A few weeks later it appeared that the baby a young couple was joyfully expecting had died a day before her birth. And a few weeks later, our sister with terminal cancer was taken up into glory.

This was a challenging period for our congregation. As pastor I was intensely involved with each of these deaths. As fruit of going through this period of loss and grief I wrote forty meditations on forty comforting texts in the Bible. I added an introduction to these meditations in which I made some general comments about grief, grieving, and comfort to guide the reader through the labyrinth of grief.

It is my sincere desire that the Spirit of the Lord will use the words of this little book to offer support and comfort in the sad and confusing grieving process.

In Christ,
Jos Douma
Haarlem, August 2008

On Grieving and Comforting

WHAT ALL happens when a great sorrow enters your life? How do you actually mourn? How can I comfort and allow myself to be comforted? During a grieving process you search for answers to these kinds of questions.

LABYRINTH

For this little book I chose the image of a labyrinth. I discovered it in a book written by Wim ter Horst entitled *On Comforting and Sorrow*. He states that grieving is not so much a process in phases (even though that approach offers insight) as it is a struggle with grief in a place where you do not know your way around nor how to get out. He uses the word *labyrinth* to describe this struggle. In a labyrinth you do not know your way around. A labyrinth is so confusing that you really do not know which way to go nor when you will finally get out. In a labyrinth you often end up at the same place because you have been walking in circles.

I noticed that this image helps those who grieve to understand a little bit about what is going on in their life. Obviously the image does not change their situation (which is still very confusing), but it does shed new light on everything happening to them and everything they feel seems to belong to it.

The main goal of this little book is to offer spiritual guidance by way of forty short meditations on forty texts from the Bible in order to persevere in the labyrinth. During the first forty days try to find a quiet place to rest and allow God to speak to you through each biblical text and its accompanying meditation. You can take time to reflect, receive a bit of light and new hope, but also experience your real sorrow as you can always take this to the Lord.

THE GRIEVING PROCESS

Even though I find the image of a labyrinth does the most justice to the grieving process, I would like to share with you some thoughts that deal with grief in phases or as tasks. Since you can become thoroughly acquainted with these models through various books and Websites, I will be brief in this introduction.

When you get news that you will not get better or that your loved one has just died, you begin to experience an incredible amount of different feelings. To be sure, every situation is different and every person reacts differently. Nevertheless, most people experience some of these different feelings and reactions: feelings of emptiness and desertion; feelings of anxiety and desperation; feelings of bewilderment, helplessness, and confusion; feelings of anger and guilt. However, it can also happen that you feel nothing, are in shock, or try to suppress your feelings by busying yourself with all sorts of things. What you experience can be very powerful and it can completely overwhelm you, especially if it is the first time you experience something like this.

These feelings and reactions are very trying: how do you know whether your experience is normal? Is it normal that you can't sleep, that the inside of your head is in chaos, that you have really awful dreams, that you apathetically stare into the distance, and that you feel almost incapable of doing things you once thought were a cinch? And is it normal that the feelings of grief can overwhelm you at the strangest moments and that you feel you cannot control them? Is it normal to feel so awfully depressed and tired? It's not funny. In fact, it's awful. But this is the way it goes when you're in a process that we call grieving.

GRIEVING: FIVE PHASES

To get more insight into the grieving process (or offer comfort in this process) one would do well to know something about the five phases that can be distinguished in the grieving process first introduced by Elisabeth Kübler-Ross in her 1969 book, *On Death and Dying*. These phases do not always neatly follow each other phase by phase, but can confusingly occur at the same time.

Phase 1: Denial. You don't want to believe what has happened. You cannot believe it. You're in a state of shock. You're out of touch with reality.

Phase 2: Anger. You get angry with the deceased who left you in the lurch. You get angry at the doctor who misdiagnosed. You get angry with yourself because you didn't notice what was happening.

Phase 3: Bargaining. When you notice that getting angry does not help, you start setting goals and making promises: "If I could only be able to speak with him one more time" or "If I could have five more minutes with her." You also find yourself bargaining with God in prayer by making promises or setting down certain conditions.

Phase 4: Depression. You feel powerless. You seclude yourself from society. You withdraw into yourself and think: "Just leave me alone."

Phase 5: Acceptance. After a period of emotional upheaval, you finally find a certain rest. You begin to enjoy things again. You begin to take initiatives. The emptiness remains, but it is integrated into a life you are busy rebuilding.

Once again: these phases do not necessarily come in the order noted above. You may find yourself lapsing into an earlier phase or moving on to a new one quite quickly. Moreover, the length of the grieving process often depends upon the intensity of the loss.

GRIEVING: FOUR TASKS

There is another approach to grieving that is quite helpful. This approach states that those who grieve face four tasks:

Task 1: Accept the reality of the loss. You will have to come full face with the reality of the loss. First, you only acknowledge it with your head. Slowly, however, you also begin to "know" it with your emotions. You need to accept that you will never see the other person again on earth and that life will never be the same again.

Task 2: Work through the pain and grief. It is absolutely necessary to acknowledge the pain and grief. If you suppress it, it will reappear in a later phase of your life. Thus, you need to take time for this "task."

Task 3: Adjust to the new environment in which the deceased is missing. You need to orient yourself to what has changed. You need to build new patterns for your life and perhaps take on new roles.

Task 4: Emotionally relocate the deceased and move on. People used to think that a healthy grieving process required you to give up your relationship with the deceased as quickly as possible. Now we know how important it is to give the deceased an appropriate place in your emotional life while you continue to rebuild your new life.

It is significant that this approach speaks about grief tasks. Processing grief is a real task. It requires hard work and costs time and energy. That's why it is important that you do not simply move on as if nothing has changed. Everything really has changed!

OFFERING COMFORT

In the grieving process you long for comfort. But what does offering comfort actually look like? Experience has taught us that when you grieve the loss of a loved one, there are always people who, with the best intentions, aggravate your pain by not taking it seriously. They come to you with well-meant advice such as, "Why don't you take a week off. That will really make you feel better." Or they begin to tell you about their own grief. Or they say, "Come on, every cloud has a silver lining." Or "Yes, you have suffered a great loss, but be sure to count your blessings!" That's not offering comfort. When that happens to you, you can feel left in the lurch.

But if this is not offering comfort, what is? That's an important question if you are longing for comfort or if you want to offer comfort. I would like to summarize what offering comfort is in the following way:

First: offer nearness.

Second: offer nearness.

Third: offer nearness.

Fourth: offer perspective.

As you can see, all the emphasis falls on nearness. It is essential that those who grieve feel accepted in their grief. Nearness is something you offer by listening to the other. Listen to their stories, their memories, their pain, their grief, and their complaints. Nearness is something you offer by empathizing and sympathizing with the other. Experience their emptiness by empathizing with the pain of this emptiness. Nearness is something you offer by lovingly touching the other. Sometimes the best thing is an encouraging arm on the shoulder, a soft touch of your hand, or a brief embrace.

Only then, after comfort is experienced in the form of nearness, does comfort offer perspective. At a certain moment you need to show the person something that those who grieve cannot see themselves because grief sometimes takes you in a vicious circles. If this is the case, it's important, if the other is ready, to share something about a perspective for the future, an expectation and a hope as a way through which God can draw closer to them. Then words offer comfort and articulate the nearness of the Lord.

There is not a whole lot of structure in the format of the forty meditations. You could, however, say that the first twenty offer nearness while the last twenty offer perspective.

FORTY DAYS

When you are in a grieving process, you may wonder when it will come to an end. It's hard to give a sensible answer to this question since the goal of grieving is that you live through your grief and learn to move on in a completely new situation. The loss will always be felt, but over time the intensity of the emotions will become less and less.

I now offer you this little book with meditations for forty days. You could get the impression that I am suggesting that the grieving process is completed in forty days. Obviously, this is not my intention. Experience, however, does teach that it's good to put markers on the grieving process. Many experience that the first year is a very important period with all its birthdays and other festivities that are celebrated for the first time without the presence of the deceased.

The experience of the first period of forty days has its own value. In the Bible, forty-day periods are known as periods of introspection, reflection, and isolation. I'm sure you are familiar with the word *quarantine*, which is used in the medical world. It's related to the Italian word *quaranta* meaning forty or a forty-day period of isolation. Moreover, in some cultures the first forty days form a clearly defined period in the grieving process.

In my opinion, for a good grieving process it is useful during the first forty days to intentionally create daily personal moments in which to experience the grief and to feel the loss and pain. The forty meditations in this little book are meant to help you with this.

We would rather
keep sorrow out
of our life.

Day 1

Overwhelmed with Grief

*How long must I wrestle with my thoughts and ev-
ery day have sorrow in my heart? How long will my
enemy triumph over me?*

PSALM 13:2

❧

WHEN WE experience sorrow in our life, we need to learn
how to deal with it. This is not always easy. We would
rather not suffer. We would rather not be worried. We would
rather keep sorrow out of our life. And yet, sorrow enters our
life. When that happens, it's good to take a psalm, receive God's
own word and express our sorrow to God. We may cry out to
God and ask, "How long, Lord?" We are allowed to complain to
God. He listens. He comforts. We may cry out to him when we
are overwhelmed with grief. He hears our cry. He gives security.
He is moved with compassion.

*Lord, thank you for your listening ear. Teach me to
feel my grief and to bring it to you.*

I'm allowed to cry,
to drench my pillow
with tears in the night.

DAY 2

Tears

*My eyes grow weak with sorrow; they fail because
of all my foes.*

PSALM 6:7

❧

I N DAYS of grief and sorrow, strong emotions can fill your life; perhaps stronger than you have known before. Sometimes, people may hand you a tissue to wipe your tears or you may reach for some tissue yourself because you don't want others to see your tears. When I read the Psalms, I learn that I don't have to try to hide my tears; I'm allowed to cry; and I may drench my pillow with my tears in the night. God knows all about those tears. He catches them in his bottle. It's good to cry because it shows that you are in the grip of deep sorrow.

*Lord, thank you that I am allowed to cry and that
my tears are allowed to flow. Lord, catch my tears in
your bottle and know me in my sorrow.*

*The pain remains,
but you realize
that God helps you
carry your burden.*

Day 3

Your Burden

Cast your cares on the Lord and he will sustain you;
he will never let the righteous fall.

PSALM 55:22

❦

THAT BURDEN you have to carry can be so heavy. We have the tendency to want to do this on our own and forget that we may cast our burden on the Lord. We continue to plod along ourselves and grind and cry without calling out to God. Yet there is a cordial heavenly invitation that says, "Cast your cares on the Lord!" You will notice that he supports you. Your grief will not all of a sudden disappear. The pain remains, but you will experience that God carries your burden with you. You see, God does not want you to stumble and fall. He does not want you to trip over your sorrow. Rather, he wants you to learn to trust him even in and through your grief.

Lord God, help me to cast my burden on you.
Support me. Carry my grief with me so that I do not
succumb to it.

*Lying awake at night
can be seen as
an invitation of the Spirit.*

DAY 4

Whispering His Name

*On my bed I remember you; I think of you through
the watches of the night.*

PSALM 63:6

❧

WHEN YOU are sick or experience tremendous grief, then
you think of all sorts of things as you lie on your bed.
You think about your cares, your difficulties, your hope, and your
hopelessness. It's all there and floating through your head and
heart. When that happens, you can start to think about God and
focus your heart on him. Lying awake at night can be seen as
an invitation of the Spirit to let go of your cares and to focus
yourself on the Lord by softly and lovingly whispering his name
and seeking his presence: Jesus. Shepherd. Rock. Savior.

*Lord, I want to whisper your name for your name is
an indication of your presence. I'm going to whisper
the name Jesus.*

We are not helpless
victims of our feelings
of grief and unrest.

Day 5

Downcast and Disturbed

Why are you downcast, O my soul? Why so disturbed within me? Put your hope in God, for I will yet praise him, my Savior and my God.

PSALM 42:5

IN THE Psalms you will notice that the psalmist often addresses the soul. The soul is our inner self, the place of our emotions, the place where the Spirit of God touches our life. You can speak to your soul and tell it to settle down, so to speak, for we are not helpless victims of our feelings of grief and unrest. We can speak to our soul and say, "Hope in God. Come on. Put your hope in God." When we do, some of that light that is often better seen in the darkness will begin to dawn in our souls. And we begin to rejoice a bit because we experience that God sees and saves us.

Lord, teach me to speak to my soul. Teach me to hope in you. I do hope in you, God. You see and save me.

At God's side
is a haven
where you are safe
and loved.

DAY 6

Eternal Pleasures at Your Right Hand

*You have made known to me the path of life; you
will fill me with joy in your presence, with eternal
pleasures at your right hand.*

PSALM 16:11

❧

WHEN WE wrestle with death that enters our life or when we
are burdened with grief because of the death of a loved
one, then the way we have to go is the way of life. God himself
points us to that way. That's why it is so important to turn to him
in your fear of death or your deep sorrow because there is no
joy in your pain and grief. Quite the opposite. But your pain and
grief are an invitation to discover that there is an abundance of
joy in the presence of God. At his side is a haven where you are
safe and loved. There you experience his continual attention for
that unique person that you are.

*Lord, show me the way of life. Teach me to discover
those eternal pleasures at your right hand. Teach me
to dwell in your presence.*

*God's presence
is deeper
than the deepest darkness.*

Day 7

In a Valley of Deep Darkness

Even though I walk through the valley of the shadow of death, I will fear no evil, for you are with me; your rod and your staff, they comfort me.

Psalm 23:4

᪥

For centuries Psalm 23 has comforted people. The psalm begins with these priceless words that are continually new and whose meaning we will never exhaust: "The Lord is my shepherd." It's so good for the soul that this psalm puts words to our experiences in life. How good it is to realize that with the Lord as your shepherd you can say that you fear no evil. This is not a pie in the sky or closing your eyes to reality for God's presence is deeper than the deepest darkness. He is there and he is with me and with you.

Thank you, Lord, that you are with me when my life takes me through a valley of deep darkness. Please stay with me.

*It's an enormously
liberating experience
to commit your life
into God's hands.*

Day 8

My Life into Your Hands

Into your hands I commit my spirit; redeem me, O
Lord, the God of truth.

PSALM 31:5

❧

WHEN WE take our refuge with God in days of pain and grief, perhaps we learn new things about the hand of God. This hand can mean different things in our life. We often try to discern how we can recognize God's hand in the things that happen. Then we sometimes experience his hand as a punishing hand. When that is the case, God teaches us to focus our eyes on Jesus and remember that Jesus bore our punishment. On the cross, he experienced the punishing hand of God (and also his loving hand because he quotes precisely this text on the cross). Thus, we may now experience God's hand as a protecting hand. It's an enormously liberating experience to commit your life into those hands.

Lord, Father of Jesus Christ, into your hands I com-
mit my life. I trust that you will save me.

Dare to accept the darkness
as an invitation to learn
to get to know the Lord again
as your light.

Day 9

Light

*The Lord is my light and my salvation—whom shall
I fear? The Lord is the stronghold of my life—of
whom shall I be afraid?*

PSALM 27:1

❧

WHEN YOUR life takes you through a dark valley, you need
some bright spots, such as a loving word, a tender touch,
a card from someone that you had not expected. It's even nicer
if in the darkness you learn to see the light again because when
everything is light around you it can sometimes be difficult to
realize just how much you need the light. Thus, dare to accept the
darkness as an invitation to learn to get to know the Lord again
as your light. His light enables you to let go of your anxiety and
experience peace. The Lord is your light. Don't be afraid!

*Lord, Father of the light, thank you that in the dark-
ness I may learn to focus on your light that gives
safety.*

*Jesus knows
this suffering
from the inside out.*

Day 10

Wounded

But he was pierced for our transgressions, he was crushed for our iniquities; the punishment that brought us peace was upon him, and by his wounds we are healed.

❧

OUR SUFFERING, our pain, our grief, our wounds are all invitations to get to know Jesus as our wounded healer. To be sure, Jesus bore our wounds as a punishment for our sins. Our wounds belong to the suffering to which creation has been subjected. They are not a punishment from God because God already punished Jesus. Jesus' wounds teach us a lot about himself. They teach us that he is not a spectator who looks at our suffering from a distance. On the contrary, he knows this suffering from the inside out. When someone who is perfectly healthy says to you that all will be well, that sounds so much different than when a fellow sufferer tells you this. Jesus is our wounded healer.

Thank you, Lord Jesus, for your wounds. Thank you that you know my wounds. Please heal me.

*Jesus
cries out the anguish
that also confronts us
today.*

Day 11

I Cry Out!

My God, my God, why have you forsaken me? Why
are you so far from saving me, so far from the words
of my groaning?

Psalm 22:1

❧

The most well known words Jesus uttered on the cross are
words he found in the Psalms. The Son of God utters human
words that are centuries old when he is about to die. He cries
out the anguish that also confronts us today. Yet his need was
different than ours. When in our grief and pain we feel that God
forsakes us, then that feeling is real, but the reality is different.
God has not forsaken us, but is with us. God really forsook Jesus.
God was not there for him. This happened so that God would
never forsake us.

God, in my forsakenness, teach me to focus on Jesus,
who was forsaken by you so that I would live.

No matter how intensely
you are troubled
by concerns
you can also
find joy in your soul.

Day 12

Your Consolation

When anxiety was great within me, your consolation brought joy to my soul.

PSALM 94:19

❧

A LOT of things can happen in your life that are cause for great concern, such as concerns about your health, your future, your loneliness, or your having to continue after a loss. Those concerns can overwhelm you to the extent that you feel you are about to drown in them. It's a great privilege that in times like these you have the courage to seek the consolation of God's unconditional presence. No matter how intensely you are troubled by these concerns you can also find joy in your soul. In other words, you find your joy not in your outward circumstances but in God's comforting security.

Lord God, teach me to seek your comfort and in the midst of much sorrow in my soul to taste your joy.

Dare to be defenseless
and he will run
to your help.

DAY 13

You See the Grief

But you, O God, do see trouble and grief; you consider it to take it in hand. The victim commits himself to you; you are the helper of the fatherless.

PSALM 10:14

❧

THE GOD of the Bible is a God who pays special attention to defenseless people. Time and again you notice that this is also the case in Jesus' life as you see him paying attention to the weak and poor. When you experience grief, feel miserable, feel defenseless because of a loss you have suffered, then know that the Lord sees your pain and trouble. He weighs it in his hand; he knows it and does not pass it by. You can trust that God will not let you go but comes to your help. So, dare to be defenseless and he will run to your help.

Thank you, Lord, that in my grief and pain I can be defenseless because you see it and are ready to come to my help.

God will not let you go.
He is your rock.
He will not let you
succumb under
your burden.

Day 14

The Rock of My Existence

My flesh and my heart may fail, but God is the
strength of my heart and my portion forever.

PSALM 73:26

❧

WHEN EVERYTHING in your life teeters and you have the
feeling that you are about to collapse because of your
trouble and grief, then it is so uplifting to hear that there still
is solid ground beneath your feet. You see, God is a rock. His
faithfulness is always firm. His involvement in your life never
changes. It's good to let that make an impact upon you and to
picture God in front of you as a rock in breakers, an immovable
stone you can stand or lie on, a rock-solid foundation under your
existence. That's what God is like. He will not let you go. He is
your rock. He will not let you succumb under your burden.

Lord God, thank you that I may know you as the
faithful rock of my existence.

*Christ's glory
is greater
than your suffering.*

DAY 15

The Suffering and the Glory

I consider that our present sufferingsare not worth
comparing with the glory that will be revealed in us.

ROMANS 8:18

❧

WHEN YOU personally experience the sufferings that be-
longs to this life, then it's not easy to relativize them. Yet,
this is precisely what Paul does. He looks at the suffering of this
present time in relation to the glory that is to come. And this
is not any easy thing for Paul to do because he himself experienced a lot of suffering. That's why it's worth your while to listen
to him and then, without denying your suffering, to open the
eyes of your heart to the glory that will be revealed to us. It's
the glory of Christ: his overwhelming glory, his radiant light, his
endless mercy. Be convinced that this glory is greater than your
suffering.

Lord God, teach me to see your glory in the midst of my
suffering so that your light penetrates my darkness.

*We are not alone
in our weakness.
Never.*

Day 16

The Spirit Groans

In the same way, the Spirit helps us in our weakness. We do not know what we ought to pray for, but the Spirit himself intercedes for us with groans that words cannot express.

ROMANS 8:26

෴

WE ARE not alone in our weakness. Never. It may feel like this sometimes because pain and grief and suffering can bring a deep loneliness into our life. Yet we are never alone because the Spirit is always with us. He is our helper in our weakness, especially when it concerns our praying. When we cannot find any words, when we are too tired to pray, when we cannot organize our thoughts because we feel so confused in our head, then the Spirit is there. And he himself intercedes for us with sighs to deep for words; the work of the Spirit also includes his sighing for us without words so that our suffering is made known to God.

Holy Spirit, what a privilege that you do not leave me alone. Thank you that you sigh for me when I have no words to pray.

*Your deepest need
is an invitation
to look to Jesus!*

Day 17

Nothing Can Separate Us from God's Love

For I am convinced that neither death nor life, neither angels nor demons, neither the present nor the future, nor any powers, neither height nor depth, nor anything else in all creation, will be able to separate us from the love of God that is in Christ Jesus our Lord.

Romans 8:38–39

❧

LET THESE words from that majestic eighth chapter of Romans make a deep impact upon you! In our suffering and sighing, in our loneliness and our grief, we can easily get the feeling that we really are alone and forsaken, even by God. Yet, with Paul, we may once again become convinced that this is not so. Nothing we experience, nothing that happens around us and to us, nothing that concerns us so much—none of that can separate us from the eternal and unconditional love we know in Christ Jesus our Lord. Thus, your deepest need is an invitation to look to Jesus!

Lord God, I want to see you in your Son.
Teach me to believe and experience that your love
will never let me go.

*Whoever
lives in darkness
may perchance
see the light.*

DAY 18

Living in Darkness

*Nevertheless, there will be no more gloom for those
who were in distress. In the past he humbled the land
of Zebulun and the land of Naphtali, but in the future he will honor Galilee of the Gentiles, by the way
of the sea, along the Jordan.*

ISAIAH 9:1

❧

THESE ARE such hopeful words. They speak about a bright
light that shines. Almost automatically my thoughts go to
Christ, who calls himself the light of the world. But what also
makes an impact upon me is that, once again, words that speak
about darkness can dominate our life. One day this may be the
darkness of failure, sin, and guilt. Another day it may the darkness of pain and grief, forsakenness and anxiety. But precisely
then, when we grope in the darkness and feel so lost, precisely
then we need to look to the bright light that is shining. Whoever
lives in darkness may perchance see the light, perhaps even more
than someone who lives in the light.

*Lord God, in the darkness I want to learn to look
to you. Surprise me with the light that is shining
so brightly.*

The Lord
does not break you
when you are bruised,
nor does he snuff you out
when you are smoldering.

Day 19

Bruised and Smoldering

A bruised reed he will not break, and a smoldering wick he will not snuff out. In faithfulness he will bring forth justice.

ISAIAH 42:3

❦

SOMETIMES CHRISTIANS ask themselves whether or not they are good believers when they feel sad and depressed. Is it right that I do not feel the joy of faith now that I am going through such a valley of deep darkness? Shouldn't I learn to be stronger in my faith? Do I trust enough in the Holy Spirit? These are questions someone asks who feels like a bruised reed or a smoldering wick. What does the Lord do with this? Does he ask questions, such as, why you are bruised? Why is the fire in your life smoldering and not burning brighter? No! Isaiah tells us very simply and in a straightforward manner that the Lord does not break you when you are bruised, nor does he snuff you out when you are smoldering. Full of compassion, he is there for you.

Lord, thank you for your compassion and patience.
Teach me to entrust myself to you.

Precisely
when you feel crushed
in spirit
the Lord is with you,
desiring
that your spirit
begin to live again.

Day 20

Crushed in Spirit

For this is what the high and lofty One says—he who lives forever, whose name is holy: "I live in a high and holy place, but also with him who is contrite and lowly in spirit, to revive the spirit of the lowly and to revive the heart of the contrite."

ISAIAH 57:15

❧

OUR GOD is a great and holy God who lives in a high and holy place. Because this is so, you might be inclined to wonder whether he is even interested in your life and in your sorrow and your feelings of being so crushed in spirit. The answer is a resounding Yes! He himself says he lives in a high and holy place with those who are low-spirited and spirit-crushed because he wants the life that fills him to also fill us. Precisely when you feel crushed in spirit the Lord is with you, desiring that your spirit begin to live again. Our holy God always sees you. He wants to be with you and enable you to experience life by being in his presence.

Lord, holy and majestic God, thank you that you live with those who are crushed in spirit. Please revive my crushed spirit.

Our sorrow and loneliness
in one way or another
have a place
in the way God travels with us
as his beloved children.

DAY 21

All Things Work Together for Good

*And we know that in all things God works for the
good of those who love him, who have been called
according to his purpose.*

ROMANS 8:28

⁂

IF WE want to learn to accept our pain here on earth then it's
important to look for God's way in our life. Paul, who himself
experienced a lot of setbacks and disappointments in his life,
teaches us to believe that everything that happens in our life
works together for good. This good is learning to live with Christ
in the Father through the Holy Spirit. In addition, our sorrow
and loneliness in one way or another have a place in the way God
travels with us as his beloved children. The reason certain things
happen often evades us, but the purpose they can achieve does
become visible. We are drawn closer to God, we grow in our surrender to Christ and experience the guidance of the Holy Spirit
in a new and deeper way.

*Father in heaven, teach me to believe that my sor-
row and pain contribute to the good you want to
do in my life.*

*We may learn to see
the suffering in our life
as the pruning
the Lord is busy with
so that we bear
more fruit.*

Day 22

Pruning and Bearing Fruit

I am the true vine, and my Father is the gardener. He cuts off every branch in me that bears no fruit, while every branch that does bear fruit he prunes so that it will be even more fruitful.

JOHN 15:1–2

❧

God, who is our Father, desires that we bear fruit in our life. He wants our life to flourish and blossom for him. This is the point Jesus makes when he says that he is the true vine and his Father is the gardener. We are the branches. This means that we may learn to see the suffering in our life as the pruning the Lord is busy with so that we bear more fruit. For instance, sometimes the Lord prunes so that we grow in patience, compassion, self-control, or other fruit of the Spirit. But the Lord also prunes so that in our disappointments we learn to witness to the presence and faithfulness of God so that others are also able to catch a glimpse of him. God prunes so that you grow. This happens when you are connected to Jesus through faith.

Lord, teach me to see that the pruning that is now taking place in my life is meant to make me grow.

If we want to follow Jesus,
our life, like a kernel of grain,
will also have to be put
into the ground and die,
because only in this way
will we be able
to bear fruit.

Day 23

A Kernel of Wheat

I tell you the truth, unless a kernel of wheat falls to
the ground and dies, it remains only a single seed.
But if it dies, it produces many seeds.

John 12:24

❧

W HEN JESUS utters these words, he is speaking about
profound things. He is first speaking about himself and
about the way he has to go. He is the kernel of wheat that falls
to the ground and dies his death on the cross, but that will bear
much fruit with his resurrection from the dead. But Jesus is also
speaking about us, his followers. If we want to follow Jesus, our
life will also have to fall to the ground and die because this is the
only way for us to bear fruit. This truth hurts, but at the same
time it teaches us to bear our pain because it has a place in God's
kingdom, and in his kingdom Jesus wants us to bear fruit.

Lord Jesus, your words about the kernel of wheat
are not easy to accept. Please help me so that I may
bear much fruit.

Is death any different than being perfectly and eternally in the presence of Christ?

Day 24

Christ in Life and Death

For to me, to live is Christ and to die is gain.

PHILIPPIANS 1:21

❧

PAUL IS the one who writes these words. Since his encounter on the way to Damascus, his life has become full of Christ. He serves Christ with heart and soul. This is the joy of his life. Christ is the joy of his life! How is this with me? Am I able to say what he says: Christ is my life? We sometimes say: my house is my life, my hobby is my life, my family is my life. What would it be like if we said that Christ is our life? This was a reality for Paul. That also explains why he sees death as gain. Is death any different than being perfectly and eternally in the presence of Christ?

Lord, teach me to also say, especially in days of pain and sorrow, that you are my life and that death is gain.

*I can do everything
through Christ,
who gives me strength
to continue on.*

Day 25

Being Able to Do Everything

I can do everything
through him who gives me strength.

PHILIPPIANS 4:13

❧

P AUL HAS great confidence in his Lord. In his life as an apostle of Christ he has had to endure many setbacks. He knows what it is to be in need, to suffer hunger and thirst, and to be deprived of sleep. He has enemies who slander and mock him. He is acquainted with physical difficulties. He has been beaten and whipped. He has been in prison. And he has continual concerns for people he feels responsible for. Yet in the midst of all of this, he says, "I can do everything through him who gives me strength." Christ is my life and my strength. He is the way that I can go on.

Lord Jesus, walking in the footsteps of Paul, teach me
to trust in the strength you give me.

*The circumstances of life
should not be the source of our joy,
but it should be knowing Jesus.*

Day 26

Always Rejoicing?

Rejoice in the Lord always.
I will say it again: Rejoice!

Philippians 4:4

⁂

How can Paul say this? Isn't it cruel to listen to this when you are going through a deep and dark valley, when your life is characterized by pain and sorrow, when one disappointment follows the other? Yes, this message is cruel if it means that you have to derive your joy from the circumstances of your life. But Paul means something else. He encourages us to seek our joy in the Lord. The circumstances of life should not be the source of our joy, but it should be knowing Jesus. Paul is talking about the joy and peace we can always experience in our hearts, even in the bitterest circumstances.

Lord, teach me not to seek my joy in the circumstances of my life, but only in you.

Everything
is preceded by the fact
that our God
wants to bless us
with his grace and peace.

Day 27

Grace and Peace

*Grace and peace to you from God our Father
and the Lord Jesus Christ.*

<small>PHILIPPIANS 1:2</small>

❦

W<small>E SHOULD</small> allow these words of grace and peace that we find at the beginning of many letters in the New Testament to speak to us at the beginning of each new day. No matter how the day turns out, no matter how you feel, no matter how much pain and loneliness you may experience in that day, all of this is preceded by the fact that our God wants to bless us with his grace and peace. *Grace* means that he, as a giving God, wants the best for you. He wants to give you his healing and forgiving presence. *Peace* means that he, as the God of shalom, wants you to experience his wholeness. Because he gives it to you, take it with both hands.

*Thank you, Lord, that in Christ you are also for me
the God of grace and peace.*

Dying
is coming to life in God.
Living
is dying to myself.

DAY 28

I Am the Life

Jesus said to her, "I am the resurrection and the life.
He who believes in me will live, even though he dies;
and whoever lives and believes in me will never die.
Do you believe this?"

JOHN 11:25–26

❧

I T IS important to continually listen very closely to the words
Jesus speaks because all the voices around and in us can so
easily drown out the voice of the Son of God. At this moment,
Jesus is saying to you and me that he is the life. He not only has
life, he not only gives life, but he is the personification of life.
When I learn to believe that again, when I allow that voice to
penetrate deeply into my soul, then I can breathe again in the
midst of pain and death and barrenness. Dying is coming to life
in God. Living is dying to myself. It's all about Jesus, who arose
for us as the true life.

Lord Jesus, speak these powerful words in my heart
and teach me to believe in you.

Jesus is the way,
the only way
we can travel
when we feel lost
in our feelings and
thoughts of grief.

Day 29

I Am the Way

Jesus answered, "I am the way and the truth and the life. No one comes to the Father except through me."

JOHN 14:6

❧

I F THERE ever is a time we need to know God as Father, then it is in a period of pain and suffering. Jesus tells us that he is the way to the Father. Only through him can we come to the Father and have him embrace us the way we embrace children. The way we need to go in such a difficult period is therefore ultimately very clear. We need to find Jesus and embrace the Father through him. Jesus' whole life is an invitation to come to him. He is the way, the only way we can travel when we feel lost in our feelings and thoughts of grief. Travel that road and find the Father.

Lord Jesus, you are my way. Teach me to come to the Father through you.

Jesus wants to lead us
through the valley of darkness
(with which he is all too familiar)
to the light.

DAY 30

I Am the Good Shepherd

I am the good shepherd;
I know my sheep and my sheep know me.

JOHN 10:14

❦

"THE LORD is my shepherd, I shall lack nothing." Generations of believers have fallen back on these words from Psalm 23 when they went through a dark valley and were looking for comfort. Ultimately Jesus is the face and content of this psalm. He is the good shepherd. He gave us everything, even his own life. As a shepherd he suffered for us so that he could help us in our suffering. He knows us as his sheep. And this is the invitation that reverberates in Jesus' words: know him as your shepherd because Jesus wants to lead us through the valley of darkness (with which he is all too familiar) to the light.

Lord Jesus, good shepherd, thank you that you know
me. I want to know you and ask you to travel with
me through the dark valley.

Our sorrow
is a powerful invitation
to focus our attention
on Jesus.

Day 31

Mourners Are Comforted

Blessed are those who mourn,
for they will be comforted.

Matthew 5:4

❧

Jesus begins his Sermon on the Mount with beatitudes. But who are the ones who are blessed? We would expect those who are happy, those who are prosperous, those who are successful in life and are not confronted with suffering. But in the kingdom of God that is coming into the world through Jesus, things are different. There you are blessed if you mourn. Why? I think because our sorrow is a powerful invitation to focus our attention on Jesus, to seek comfort where it can only be found, namely, with the Lord. You are really happy only if you are and remain connected to him.

Lord Jesus, teach me to experience my sorrow as an
invitation to seek comfort and happiness with you.

Jesus invites you
and challenges you,
especially when you
are experiencing darkness,
to put your trust
in the light.

Day 32

Trust in the Light

"Put your trust in the light while you have it, so that you may become sons of light." When he had finished speaking, Jesus left and hid himself from them.

John 12:36

❧

I T IS not easy to believe in the light when you are walking in darkness. Darkness can be so overwhelming, can be so oppressive, can feel so omnipresent that it almost seems incredible there would be light. Jesus speaks these words about light just before his death, when he is still here one earth as a human being. Now, however, we can know him as the resurrected One, the One who brought us the light by going through the darkness. In fact, now Jesus is the light of the world. He invites you and challenges you, especially when you are experiencing darkness, to put your trust in the light. If you do, you are a child of the light.

Lord Jesus, teach me to put my trust in the light and to confidently surrender myself to you.

We may bring every burden
that oppresses us to him.
When we do,
he will exchange it
with peace.

Day 33

Come to Jesus

Come to me, all you who are weary and burdened,
and I will give you rest.

MATTHEW 11:28

❧

JESUS KNOWS what lives in our hearts. He got to know this from the inside out when he was on earth as a human being. He knows the burdens we carry, the fatigue that oppresses us, the despair we feel because we see no way out anymore. He is acquainted with all of this. In fact, he took all our weariness and burdens upon himself. This Jesus says to us today: Come to Me! We may bring every burden that oppresses us to him. When we do, he will exchange it with peace. This does not mean that our circumstances immediately change. But our heart does! A peace and wholeness enters into our hearts that chases the restlessness away.

Jesus, teach me to accept your loving invitation
to find rest in you.

A time will really come
when all the tears
we shed in this world
will be wiped away.

Day 34

No More Tears

*He will wipe every tear from their eyes. There will be
no more death or mourning or crying or pain, for the
old order of things has passed away.*

REVELATION 21:4

❧

WHEN YOU are tied to a bed because you are sick, then
your world can become very small. In fact, sometimes
your world is not much bigger than your bed. When you are
tormented by concerns and sorrow, often the same happens.
You are withdrawn into a small circle. At times like these it is
so beneficial when someone opens up another perspective for
you, such as a perspective towards the future. You see, a time will
really come when all the tears that we shed in this world will be
wiped away by the Lord himself! A moment will arrive when all
that overpowers and overshadows so much today will be gone.
Just imagine that moment. Try it. Let the Spirit lead you.

*Lord, I am trying to imagine that grand moment
when I will never cry again. Allow me to experience
now some of that future joy.*

A completely new reality
full of love and life,
full of grace and goodness,
full of joy and peace
will dawn.

Day 35

Everything New

*He who was seated on the throne said, "I am making
everything new!" Then he said, "Write this down, for
these words are trustworthy and true."*

REVELATION 21:5

❧

THE BOOK of Revelation gives us a glimpse of heaven and
a foretaste of how things will be later when all pain and
sorrow belong to the past. Jesus, who sits upon the throne, puts
words to this glorious reality. He doesn't use many words, but the
words he does use encompass much. Actually, they encompass
everything, because he is not just going to make some things
new, but everything! A completely new reality full of love and
life, full of grace and goodness, full of joy and peace will dawn.
Everything will be new because everything that is old will be
gone. Everything will be new, completely new, just like Jesus.

*Lord Jesus, I thank you out of the bottom of my heart
that you are going to make all things new.*

Ultimately,
life in the kingdom of God
to which we as Christians belong
is not about this earthly life,
but about eternal life.

Day 36

Eternal Life

Now this is eternal life: that they may know you, the
only true God, and Jesus Christ,
whom you have sent.

JOHN 17:3

⌘

S OMETIMES WE are so tied to life on this earth that it looks as
if this life is eternal life. But that is not so because this earthly
life is temporary. All joy and success in this life is temporary just
as all sorrow and disappointment. Ultimately life in the kingdom
of God to which we as Christians belong is not about this earthly
life, but about eternal life. And this eternal life begins now already, here on this earth. When we know the only true God and
his Son Jesus Christ, then we have eternal life. Do you know Jesus
Christ? Do you love him? Do you know that he loves you? Are
you accepting his love? If so, then you have eternal life!

Lord Jesus, thank you that I may discover that know-
ing you and your Father means having eternal life!

He surrounds me
in my sorrow and pain;
it's like an eternal embrace
from the Almighty.

DAY 37

Alpha and Omega

"I am the Alpha and the Omega," says the Lord God,
"who is, and who was, and who is to come,
the Almighty."

REVELATION 1:8

❧

THE LORD Jesus Christ embraces our life. He is there at the beginning of our life as the Alpha, the One who always was there, long before I was born. He is there at the end of our life as the Omega, the last One who will always be there, far beyond my death. He surrounds me in my sorrow and pain; it's like an eternal embrace from the Almighty. He carries me. My suffering is part of the suffering of this world. This suffering, in turn, is embedded in the eternal faithfulness of the Almighty. I drink in his words and allow them to enter deeply into my heart. I experience a peace and wholeness in this gracious embrace because Jesus is the Alpha and the Omega.

Lord Jesus, thank you that you are there both in the
beginning and the end. May I experience that you
eternally embrace me.

We don't see this,
we don't understand this,
but we believe.

DAY 38

Faith Remains

And now these three remain: faith, hope and love.
But the greatest of these is love.

1 CORINTHIANS 13:13

❧

WITH EVERYTHING that falls away, with every loss we suffer, faith remains. This is God's promise. Believing is being convinced of the truth of what we do not see. For instance, we do not see that ultimately life is good when the Lord is present. Or we do not see that what no mind has conceived is really true, namely, that an eternal and perfect life is awaiting us. We don't see this, we don't understand this, but we believe. We entrust ourselves to the God we have come to know in Jesus as the Lord, who is faithful to his word and in whom there is an overabundance of love. He gave his life for us. We believe this.

Lord God, thank you that we can continue to believe
in days of pain and loss. I believe.
Please help my unbelief.

*We focus
the eyes of our hearts
on the future,
and we see Jesus Christ.
He inspires hope
because he
will one day
return.*

Day 39

Hope Remains

And now these three remain: faith, hope and love.
But the greatest of these is love.

1 Corinthians 13:13

❧

According to a well-known saying, where there is hope there is life. This is quite biblical for hope is focused on the future. When we hope, we distance ourselves from the present circumstances of our life that can sometimes be so oppressive and depressing. We focus the eyes of our hearts on the future, and we see Jesus Christ. He inspires hope because he will one day return. "I am coming soon," he said. But our hope reaches even further than this. Jesus himself is our hope because he is our Savior. Thus, our future lies securely in his hand no matter how we may feel at the present time. Therefore, entrust yourself to him and be hopeful. He will make sure that all things turn out well.

Jesus, you are my hope. Help me to cling to you and
to entrust myself to your future.

In the labyrinth of grief
we can be assured
of one absolute certainty:
God's divine love
has eternal value.

DAY 40

The Greatest Is Love

And now these three remain: faith, hope and love.
But the greatest of these is love.

1 CORINTHIANS 13:13

❦

SOMETIMES WE think that our sorrow or pain or loss is the greatest thing in our life. But that is not true. Love is the greatest. Faith will turn into sight. Beyond all faith and unbelief we will one day see Jesus. Hope will become boundless certainty. Our expectations will be fulfilled beyond our imagination. But love remains. This love continues to exist forever: God's love in Christ, our love for him and for one another. In the labyrinth of grief we can be assured of one absolute certainty: God's love has eternal value. And where there is love there is life. Eternal life. Therefore, love with all your heart, soul, mind, and strength.

Lord, you who love me, I thank you that your love
transcends my imagination and lasts forever. Great
is your love, greater than anything else.
In Jesus' name. Amen.